PRIEST
PURGATORY

CREDITS

STORY BY:
TROY LEWTER, STU LEVY, AND
MIN-WOO HYUNG

WRITTEN BY:
TROY LEWTER AND DAN JOLLEY

PENCILS BY:
DIEGO YAPUR

PAGE LAYOUTS BY:
FERNANDO MELEK

INKS BY:
DIEGO YAPUR, FERNANDO MELEK, AND
LEANDRO RIZZO

COLORS BY:
HERNÁN CABRERA, ANDRÉS LOZANO,
RODRIGO DÍAZ, JAVIER SUPPA, AND
MBLAR STUDIO (LA PLATA)

COVER BY:
RAYMOND SWANLAND

LETTERING BY:
ERIKA TERRIQUEZ

EDITOR: TROY LEWTER

PRINT PRODUCTION MANAGER :
LUCAS RIVERA

MANAGING EDITOR: VY NGUYEN

SENIOR DESIGNER: LOUIS CSONTOS

ART DIRECTOR: AL-INSAN LASHLEY

DIRECTOR OF SALES & MANUFACTURING:
ALLYSON DE SIMONE

SENIOR VICE PRESIDENT:
MIKE KILEY

C.E.O. & CHIEF CREATIVE OFFICER:
STU LEVY

ISBN: 978-1-4278-1885-0

PRINTED IN KOREA

JUDAS

UH-RUH UH-RUH UH-
RUH UH-RUH...

UH-RUH UH-
RUH UH-RUH
UH-UHHHH...

Later...

Priest Designate DC-66. August 24.

The mission we have undertaken is so highly classified it has not even been given a name.

So far, the challenges we have faced have not been out of the ordinary...

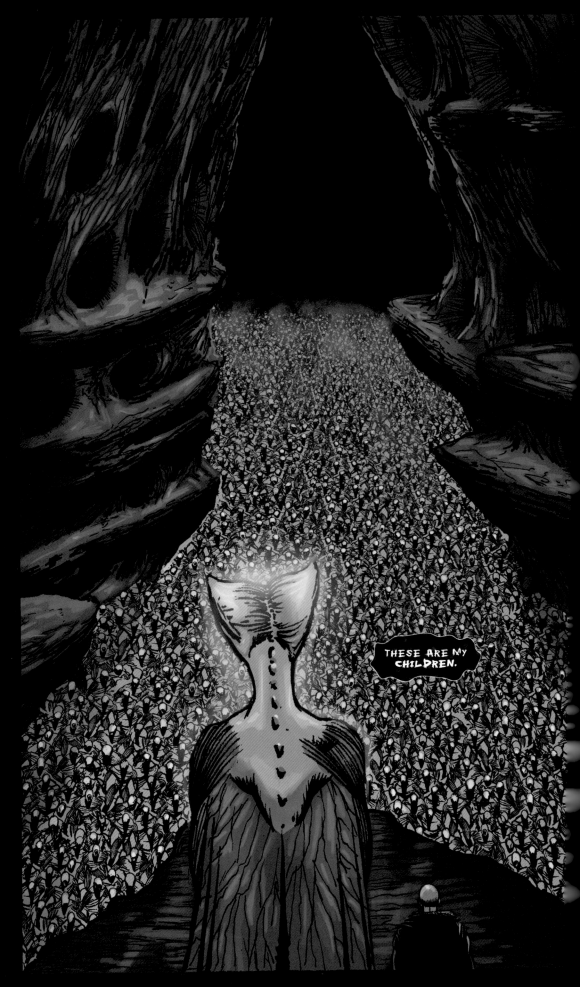

RED SEA

Sometimes I have this nightmare...

...where it feels like I'm being crushed.

SEX

And I can't _move_.

So all I can do...

...as this horrible, deadly weight begins to _crush_ me...

...is _let_ it.

GET IT OFF!!
GET IT OFF!!

YOU WOKE ME UP
FOR *THIS?*

I WAS HAVIN' MY FAVORITE
TWIN BLONDES DREAM.
SISTERS MAKIN' THEMSELVES
A *BUCK SANDWICH.*

JUST KILL IT FOR ME,
PLEASE! MY DAMN
HANDS ARE FEET ARE
TIED UP!!

OH, THAT'S HARDLY
NECESSARY.

IS IT, LITTLE
FELLOW? *IS IT?*

NO, OF COURSE
NOT...!

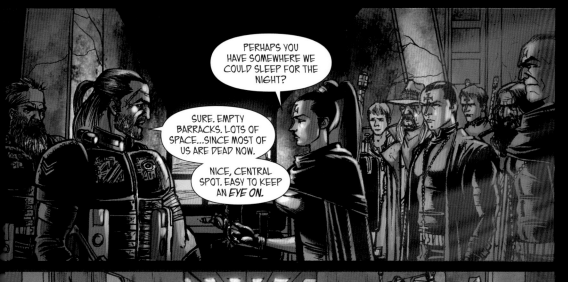

PERHAPS YOU HAVE SOMEWHERE WE COULD SLEEP FOR THE NIGHT?

SURE. EMPTY BARRACKS. LOTS OF SPACE...SINCE MOST OF US ARE DEAD NOW.

NICE, CENTRAL SPOT. EASY TO KEEP AN *EYE ON.*

"THESE MEN ARE DANGEROUS."

SHOW ME ONE IN WAR THAT ISN'T.

YOU KNOW WHAT I MEAN. THERE'S WAR CRAZY...AND THEN THERE'S *THIS.* AND THOSE SYMBOLS ON THEIR CLOTHES? SOME EVEN CARVED INTO THEIR FLESH...

YES...*UMPH*...ABOUT THAT. I'VE SEEN THEM BEFORE. INSIDE...*UNH*... DC-66'S JOURNAL...

HERE... LET ME HELP YOU WITH THAT.

...where it feels like I'm being _crushed._

THERE IS A SCRIPTURE VERSE THAT HAS ALWAYS GIVEN ME GREAT SOLACE.

IT'S WELL-KNOWN; AMONG PEOPLE WHO **KNOW** THE SCRIPTURE, IT IS AMONG THE MOST COMMON TO COMMIT TO MEMORY.

BUT EVERY SO OFTEN... SOMETHING HAPPENS. SOMETHING THAT SHAKES ME, ALL THE WAY DOWN TO MY ROOTS.

EVERYONE, WAIT A MINUTE...!

WHEN MOSES WAS FACED WITH AN INSURMOUNTABLE OBSTACLE, HE ASKED GOD TO PART THE RED SEA...

...AND THE WATERS GAVE WAY, AND MADE A PATH FOR HIM AND THE ISRAELITES. RIGHT?

WE JUST NEED TO DO THE *SAME!*

YOUR BABBLING MIGHT BE *RELEVANT*--IF THERE WERE A RIVER WITHIN *MILES* OF OUR LOCATION.

NO, *NO,* DON'T YOU GET IT? OUR SEA *IS* THE *VAMPIRES.*

AND WHILE WE DON'T HAVE MOSES'S STAFF...

BECAUSE THE **WORDS** OF THE **SCRIPTURE** HAVE COME BACK TO ME. THEY COURSE THROUGH MY MIND LIKE THE **BLOOD** IN MY **VEINS.**

THE LORD IS MY SHEPHERD; I SHALL NOT WANT.

HE MAKETH ME TO LIE DOWN IN GREEN PASTURES.

HE LEADETH ME BESIDE THE STILL WATERS.

THY ROD AND THY STAFF, THEY COMFORT ME.

THOU PREPAREST A TABLE BEFORE ME IN THE PRESENCE OF MINE ENEMIES.

THE *HONOR* IS ALL *MINE*.

THOU ANOINTEST MY HEAD WITH OIL.

MY CUP RUNNETH OVER.

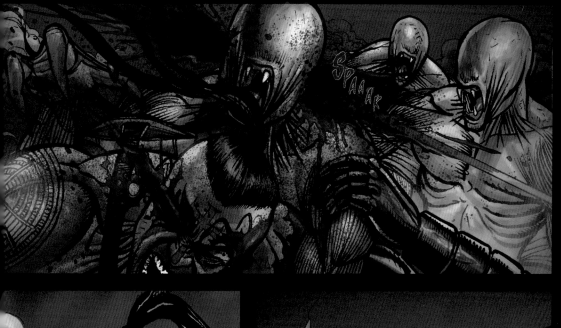

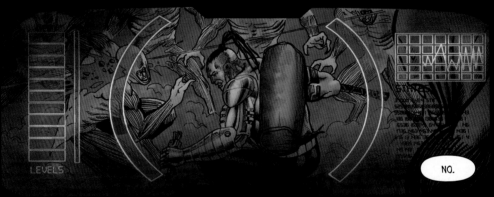

PRIE✝ST
IN 3D

REEN GEMS PRESENTS A MICHAEL DE LUCA PRODUCTIONS/STARS ROAD ENTERTAINMENT PRODUCTION IN ASSOCIATION WITH TOKYOPOP "PRIEST" PAUL BETTANY
KARL URBAN CAM GIGANDET MAGGIE Q LILY COLLINS WITH STEPHEN MOYER AND CHRISTOPHER PLUMMER MUSIC BY CHRISTOPHER YOUNG
CUTIVE GLENN S. GAINOR STEVEN H. GALLOWAY STU LEVY PRODUCED BY MICHAEL DE LUCA JOSHUA DONEN MITCHELL PECK BASED ON THE GRAPHIC NOVEL SERIES PRIEST BY MIN-WOO HYUNG
THIS FILM IS NOT YET RATED. WRITTEN BY CORY GOODMAN DIRECTED BY SCOTT STEWART SONY
FUTURE INFO GO TO FILMRATINGS.COM

IN THEATERS MAY 13
Priest-TheMovie.com